IN MY ARMS

Setareh Ebrahimi

PRESS

In My Arms

Published by Bad Betty Press
www.badbettypress.com

Cover design by Joel Auterson

Printed and bound in the United Kingdom

A CIP record of this book is available from the British Library.

ISBN: 978-1-9997147-2-7

IN MY ARMS
Setareh Ebrahimi

Setareh Ebrahimi is an Iranian-British poet, writer and artist. She was born in Brighton—where she lived for twenty years—a place that informed her work, outlook and creativity. She now works and lives in Faversham. She is an active figure in the creative writing scene in Kent, running poetry evenings and regularly performing her poetry at different events in the county, as well as the rest of the country. She has been widely published in journals and magazines such as Confluence, Brittle Star and Thanet Poetry Journal. She obtained her BA in English Literature from the University of Westminster, and her Master's in English and American Literature from The University of Kent.

Contents

Meet the Mothers

They are kind as you are sexless
when they meet you
as a soft, bounding blur.
Like angels they temporarily shade
with wing in overflow.

When you meet mothers
and they know,
eyes zeroing in in a crowd,
instigating immediate,
unspoken understanding.
Her pupil linked to mine
as if a metal line ran through both.

When you meet mothers unaware,
leaving you with debauchery
like a missed fire-swallowing trick.
When you meet mothers saving their boys,
when you meet mothers ruining them,
when you meet mothers
doing one via the other.

When you are cautious confidantes
united against the enemy,
resuscitating the land,
poised to break apart

and build barricades.

Sons grown detached
culture against community.
When you become a mother,
new with joy,
holding a toy to be broken,
or a man, a boy.

Through the Fish Tank

In the city of sin I flit
weightless as trash,
worthless and in love.

My brother in a tasseled two piece
offered me what was on his tongue
like a mother feeding her young
and the rest was fireworks,
red lips, ochre skin.

I was the knight
out of my Elvis lapels,
amongst gold teeth, Latin beats.
She was an angel in white.
Later her wings were lost
or I cast them off.

I followed the fish
till they led me to their queen
as if she were a mermaid
and now suppose she said,
"You saw me drowned."

We were happiest in water
unless we were air,
like the morning after consummation

when the bed was a cloud,
the sky a sheet I kept inflating for you,
your face the sun on the horizon.

We couldn't stay in love
any more than we could air or water,
we were flesh,
and had we been of the corrupted kind
we would have lived long,
poisonous lives like our parents,
our infections keeping us alive.

I smoke in the desert trailer,
glad to have known truth
beside open Hawaiian shirts,
snakeskin steel-capped boots,
guns with icons on,
not to see you lie cold
amongst neon crucifixes.

Yes I lied,
imitated the state in which my brother lies,
but our ancestors came from the sea,
next to which my brother cursed me,
and in my arms,
died.

Chest

Her breasts spread like eyes on butterfly wings
when they come to rest.

I scale the contours
of this pale landscape
like the misty mountains,
ecstatic at exploring alone,
a child left to play at night
too young to know death or fear.

In every marble ridge
there is a pocket to love
and fill with a dream.
The depress between ribs
is soft as bruised fruit.

With my head to this slight cage I mimic its heave
as if I were lurching on a boat.

Here I play with new,
fragile strands of emotion
like optical fibres.

Here I hear the Earth dance and skip.

In the Chain

Home glows like adverts and unfocused gold lights through a sympathetic camera.

Things are precious in the hand, taciturn, rattle them at the ear to hear the filament of a faux frost string of bulbs. One in the chain always dies.

Only the procedure is known, motion through it blind like the line after the one just sung to discover the silence in an ending.

Gold-pink cherry medicine, elixir, potion, is filling the sleek simplicity of luxury...

Nudging between the very atoms, not stopping in awe, he straddles a bubble to the top and pops, raw, a mental motion from abstraction.

A girl-woman in a red skirt has a Monroe moment.

Cake

I want to see his hands,
poised with concentration,
slightly trembling
due to alien consideration,
carefully take the brilliant knife
and slice a mathematical piece
of cake, like art.

He uses the trowel to coax it,
with barest touch, out of its slot,
maybe balancing with a fourth finger,
not wanting to make a mess, yet.
He is alone.

Those little lady hands, on a man,
their worn, crescent-moon nails.
I want to see that exquisite mouth
wrap unbearably slowly around
every bite, a fork is paramount.
How unfairly his lips are written into thought,
they must be caught in the act,
their precise shape never seen alike.

This is no shop-bought cream cheese job,
it's seen fire. Its crust
is the cooled surface of the moon,

but browning.

The rest is obscene,
stuffed down, obliterated,
spread over skin,
crumbs scattered far,
dish clean.

Buried Alive

Have you ever buried someone alive?
Have you ever lived
amongst dead men, walking, laughing,
unaware that they're ghosts,
or been a ghost yourself?

I have disregarded
all physical evidence of existence,
made trivial vital signs of life,
teased claims to pulse and breath
like knots, secretly, over time.

Have you ever buried someone
to remain above ground?
Have you ever felt your heart snap
like a ripcord
after years of stretching?

Seeing them is like a delayed hologram,
their smiles and touches are irrelevant,
received after the event.

Have you ever buried someone alive?
Have you ever seen hands
scrabbling in the earth, drowning?
Have you ever soothed the egg of the skull

with a sharp shock of the shovel,
and, afloat in the necropolis,
embraced silence?

Picture Book

Behind her the reeds grow long and lush,
pea green and angled to the left.
They're playing in front of forest-coloured tree clusters,
sprinkled together like chives on a chopping board.

Such soft shapes do not assault the eye,
I keep a folded picture of my lover in a book I'm taking
the rest of our time together to finish.
Every night I make a little progress,
dwell at the tinged crease I've let run along her length,
then read on, folding the landscape, disturbed,
a place throbs next to her like a cavity.

My fingernails are bloody from stealing this.
In spite of the crime she sits, peaceful,
an open smile dancing on her lips,
spread to show a sparkling bite.
Her bleached limbs pour down to rest,
streaked with honey coloured sun.

Her eyes are two high placed semi-circles,
curve up, noticing something away
from the bullseye of the lens.
What stalks low among the grass?
I must not invent a curse, weary
from carrying this secret weight in my book.
She is still laughing, silent.

A Ghost in Berlin

I met a ghost in Berlin,
a metalhead with the exact physique,
the same patches of shockingly dark down
secretly on his body,
the long hair, the beard,
the teeth, smile and voice,
the same blue eyes.
His hands were slightly different,
better, so worse.
I took him,
a sign, from the universe.

His soul fit the specification
of the July Irish guitarist who strummed
as I sipped Jäger.
A ghost stuffed his hands
in my mouth,
a ghost strangled me
then slept in his chains,
swatting me like a fly
as I created constellations
on his back with kisses.

I want to pass through life unnaturally:
undisturbed and not disturbing.

Release me from the drama of love
and let me be free.
Dear reader, what would you
have me do?
We are beautiful
only for being individual,
but I'm like my mother
who made me a mirror
as she waned and wasted for men.

Learning to Draw Darwin

In the beginning, evolution was not detectable.
There were lines and marks and no responsibility.
Then different shapes could be grouped.
Soon they were put together
with purpose still unfathomable,
the same unclear forms recurring.
With delight, the crudest humans emerged,
their features falling off their faces,
an eye just outside the parameter of the skull
like an accident of the womb.

This is how my sister drew
early life with terrifying care,
her hand trembled as she kept
heads attached to bodies,
bodies attached to limbs.
Man became different from woman,
then went away completely.
Our family distinguished different animals,
recognised ourselves less
through realistic representation
than the symbolic.

The figures of girls grew finer.
My own abilities were technically surpassed,
she was no longer capturing bodies but clothes,

a dull point disguised as politics,
a self-referencing, outer membrane.
The costumes become so fantastic
they obscure the humans they contain.
Perhaps she again wants abstraction, freedom.

The White Witch

Hellfire is mercy by comparison.
Burn in the cold,
turn black with frostbite.
I will be the freezing wind
you cannot grasp to punish.

Sit alone in an igloo,
eat icicles for every meal.
All day the rod bobs in the deep
but never tugs with life.
You wish an animal, even monster,
howled outside.

Bully and beat yourself,
have every point lead back to you,
try to thaw it out
with the lake's frozen reflection
over grand schematics scratched in the ice.

I am generous.
Take all the space
in the physical world
for your prison.
I will be the intangible landlord
you're dying to meet,
whispering around every corner.

Even dispersion is a skill,
anything perfected is an art.
For questions there are words without answer,
for pain there is custom without tears,
for affinity there are smiles without eyes.

People threaten death or pain,
loss of money or beauty,
all mental and material faculties
but I would say this—
enjoy the silence,
go deaf from its screams.

In the Nurse's Bed

Fashion an artificial twilight
by blending the sight of the world with a squint.
Dust motes stumble into the box room,
thoughts are sent away at the door.

Tin-packed in the bed
we keep the sacred air between us stale,
a pocket of nothing to love like a child.
The other wonders how many the one
it holds has loved:
your thirteen-split figure,
my thumb and first finger.

In the day we admit ourselves
to further institution for sleep,
whittling away the sharp edges of things,
bite and taste, growing slow and wise.
Like God we lose no moment,
sun bleached paper shells on a sand beach,
eating air and leaf with the driest of hands.

Outside the New Year's cold assaults the senses
with imposing flavour and expectation,
wanting to swell out to our edges till it becomes skin.

Wandering Rocks

So far from humanity the pace of your body slows
to that of the mountains. Last traces of civilization
claw at the ground that's cracked fresh green
and fragrant earth. An immediate open expanse
like a ripcord snapping is a sight books can't prepare for,
that feeling of knowing every dull thing outside
your house without leaving it is violated by the landscape
that's more a different planet than country.

Part Amazon, echo of oriental branches and brooks,
humid, with a silence that's natural. You're slightly dirtier
and somehow purer. Wean your body off its contraption use,
learn its self-sufficiency. In these tall forests
with their thin, dense trees intoxicated Israelis saw fairies.
You and your girlfriends are nymphs in the land of nudity
without nakedness, where mist would be seen to circle
treetops if anyone was looking, where you almost forget to be.

Acknowledgements

'Meet the Mothers' appeared in *New Writing from Postgraduate Creative Writers at Kent* in Summer 2016 from the University of Kent.

'Through the Fish Tank' appeared in audio format on the CD *Our Words on Your Lips*, a compilation of poetry from Kent poets, put out by Lenny's Studio on August 11, 2017.

'Chest' appeared in the anthology *Love's Labyrinth* published by Forward Press in January 2011.

'In the Chain' appeared in the Forward Poetry collection *A Year Gone By - A Collection of Poetry* in April 2013.

'Cake' appeared in the zine *I Speak My Truth*, put together by Sarah Holt in 2016.

'Picture Book' was included in the Spring 2013 issue of the poetry magazine *Inkapture*.

'Learning to Draw Darwin' appeared in the winter 2016-17 issue of *The Grapevine* zine.

'Wandering Rocks' was included in the Forward Press anthology, *The Great Escape - A Collection of Poetry* in January 2015.

Lightning Source UK Ltd.
Milton Keynes UK
UKOW01f2331180218
318094UK00001B/28/P